Traditional

FARMHOUSE COOKING

CHARTWELL
BOOKS, INC.

Published by Chartwell Books
a division of Book Sales, Inc.
114 Northfield Avenue
Edison, NJ 08837

This edition produced for sale
in the U.S.A., its territories
and dependencies only.

ISBN 0-7858-0422-6

Edited, designed and typeset by Haldane Mason, London

Printed in Italy

Note: Cup measurements in this book are for standard American cups. Unless otherwise stated, milk is assumed to be full-fat and pepper is freshly ground black pepper. All butter is sweet unless otherwise stated.

CONTENTS

LEEK AND POTATO SOUP

This deliciously smooth soup can be served hot in chilly weather or cold in the summer months.

SERVES ❹

2 tbsp butter

1 lb leeks, trimmed and sliced

1 onion, chopped

3½ cups chicken or vegetable stock

12 oz potatoes, peeled and cut into chunks

1 tbsp chopped fresh chives

1¼ cups milk

4 tbsp whipping cream

salt and pepper

chopped fresh chives to garnish

1 Melt the butter in a large pan and add the leeks and onion. Cook over a low heat, stirring frequently, for about 10 minutes until the vegetables are softened but not browned.

2 Add the chicken or vegetable stock, potatoes, and chives. Bring to the boil, reduce the heat, cover, and simmer gently for 20–30 minutes, until the vegetables are cooked.

3 Rub the soup through a strainer, or place in a food processor or blender and work until it is smooth. Then return it to the pan. Add the milk and reheat the soup gently over a low heat, stirring occasionally, until it is piping hot. Season to taste.

4 If you are serving the soup hot, whip the cream while the soup is reheating until the cream thickens slightly. Ladle into 4 warmed soup bowls, spoon an equal amount of

whipped cream on top of each serving and sprinkle with chopped fresh chives.

5 If serving chilled, cool the soup quickly and refrigerate for 2–3 hours until it is ice cold. Add the whipped cream and chives just before serving.

SPLIT PEA AND HAM SOUP

A bowlful of this chunky golden soup on a cold winter's day is almost a meal in itself.

SERVES ❹

2 tbsp butter or margarine

1 large onion, chopped

1 large carrot, chopped

¾ cup diced lean ham

1 tsp ground cumin

3½ cups ham or vegetable stock

⅓ cup yellow split peas

1 tbsp chopped fresh parsley

salt and pepper

sprigs of parsley to garnish

1 Melt the butter or margarine in a large pan. Add the onion and carrot and fry gently over a medium heat until the vegetables are softened, about 5 minutes.

2 Stir in the cubes of ham and the cumin and cook gently for a further 5 minutes, stirring frequently.

3 Pour in the ham or vegetable stock and add the yellow split peas. Bring to the boil, then reduce the heat. Cover and simmer the soup very gently for about 45 minutes until the peas are cooked.

4 Add the parsley to the soup and stir well. Season to taste. Ladle into warmed soup bowls and garnish with sprigs of parsley. Serve at once.

POTTED CHEESE SAVORIES

SERVES 6

½ cup butter, at room temperature

3 cups crumbled blue cheese

1 cup fresh white breadcrumbs

1 tbsp port

1 tsp chopped fresh parsley

This creamy appetizer is a must for blue-cheese lovers. If tightly wrapped and stored in the refrigerator, it will keep for up to 2 weeks.

1 Put the butter into a large mixing bowl and beat until it is softened. Add the crumbled cheese and beat together until it is creamy, but not too smooth.

2 Work the breadcrumbs into the cheese mixture, then add the port and parsley. Mix together until thoroughly combined.

3 Pack the mixture into an earthenware pot or other container. Cover and refrigerate.

4 Take the potted cheese out of the refrigerator about 30 minutes before serving to allow it to reach room temperature. Serve with crackers or fresh, crusty bread.

TWO-CHEESE RAREBIT

For a simple, filling snack, a tasty rarebit is hard to beat. Cream cheese and sharp Cheddar are combined in this recipe to give a golden bubbly topping.

SERVES 4

½ cup cream cheese

1 tbsp butter

1 cup shredded sharp Cheddar cheese

1 tsp Worcestershire sauce

1 tsp chopped fresh chives

pinch of chili powder

4 thick-cut slices bread

TO GARNISH

2 sliced tomatoes

chopped fresh chives

1 To make the rarebit mixture, put the cream cheese and butter into a large mixing bowl and beat together until blended. Add the shredded Cheddar cheese, Worcestershire sauce, chives, and chili powder, and mix well until thoroughly combined.

2 Toast the bread lightly on both sides and spread each piece with the rarebit mixture. Place under a preheated hot broiler and cook until the topping is melted and bubbling.

Watch the toast carefully as it cooks, as the cheese can burn very quickly.

3 Top each piece with tomato slices and sprinkle with the chopped chives. Serve at once.

CHEESE AND ONION PIE

The simplest of ingredients make a very tasty double-crust savory pie, delicious served with a crisp salad and sliced tomatoes.

1 Cook the onions in boiling, lightly salted water for about 10 minutes until tender. Drain thoroughly and mash with a potato masher. Add the shredded cheese and mix well. Season to taste and allow to cool.

2 Sift the flour and a pinch of salt into a large mixing bowl. Cut the butter or margarine and shortening into small pieces. Add to the flour and rub in with your fingertips until the mixture resembles fine breadcrumbs. Add enough chilled water to make a firm dough. Knead lightly for a few moments, then wrap and refrigerate for about 10 minutes.

3 Roll out half the dough on a lightly floured counter and use to line an 8 inch metal pie plate. Spoon the cheese and onion mixture on top. Roll out the remaining dough, moisten the edges with a little water and use to cover the pie. Press the edges securely together to seal, then trim and flute them. Use any leftover trimmings to make leaves

12

to decorate the top. Brush with milk to glaze.

4 Place in a preheated oven at 425°F, and bake for 10 minutes, then reduce the temperature to 375°F, and bake for a further 20–25 minutes until cooked and golden brown.

COUNTRY VEGETABLE AND BARLEY CASSEROLE

This fresh vegetable casserole makes a good accompaniment to meat or poultry, but is also a very satisfying meal by itself.

SERVES 4

1 tbsp vegetable oil

2 tbsp butter

6 oz shallots

6 oz baby carrots

6 oz baby parsnips

6 oz small turnips, quartered

12 oz small new potatoes

¼ cup pearl barley

2½ cups vegetable stock

1¼ cups dry white wine

1 tbsp chopped mixed fresh herbs

4 oz sugar snap peas or snow peas

salt and pepper

1 Heat the oil and butter in a large flameproof casserole and fry the shallots, carrots, parsnips, and turnips gently for 4–5 minutes.

2 Add the potatoes, pearl barley, vegetable stock, white wine, and chopped mixed herbs. Bring to the boil, then cover the casserole and place it in a preheated oven at 375°F. Cook for about 1 hour, adding the sugar snap peas or snow peas 20 minutes before the end of the cooking time. Season to taste just before serving.

Serve in large warmed soup bowls with some crusty bread, or as a side dish to a main meal of roast or braised meat.

CORNED BEEF HASH WITH EGGS

A quick and simple corned beef hash makes a tasty light lunch. This version uses eggs to make it more filling and nutritious.

1 Heat the vegetable oil in a large skillet and add the onions and potatoes. Fry briskly for 2–3 minutes, then reduce the heat to low and cook gently, stirring occasionally, until the potatoes are tender – about 15–20 minutes.

2 Add the corned beef hash to the pan. Stir to combine and cook gently for 5 minutes, stirring occasionally. Add Worcestershire sauce and season to taste.

3 Make 4 hollows in the potato mixture and crack an egg into each one, being careful not to break the yolks. Continue to cook gently over a low heat for 4–5 minutes, until the egg whites are cooked but the yolks are still soft.

4 Divide the hash into 4, 1 egg per portion, and use a pancake turner to lift each portion out onto a warmed serving plate. Garnish with a little chopped parsley.

BEEF AND BEER STEW WITH PARSLEY DUMPLINGS

The parsley dumplings taste just right in this delicious beef stew, but you must use fresh parsley, as dried doesn't have enough flavor.

SERVES ❹

1 tbsp vegetable oil

1½ lb lean stewing steak, cut into large chunks

2 celery stalks, chopped

1 large carrot, sliced

2 leeks, trimmed and sliced

scant 2 cups beef stock

1¼ cups light beer

salt and pepper

DUMPLINGS

1 cup self-rising flour

¼ cup margarine

1 tbsp chopped fresh parsley

1 Heat the oil in a large pan. Add the chunks of meat, a handful at a time, and cook over a high heat until they are sealed and browned. Add the celery, carrot, and leeks and cook for about 5 minutes, stirring frequently.

2 Pour in the beef stock and beer. Season to taste. Bring to the boil, then reduce the heat.

Cover and cook for about 1½–2 hours until the meat is tender.

3 To make the dumplings, sift the flour and a pinch of salt into a mixing bowl. Stir in the chopped parsley and rub in the margarine with your fingertips until the mixture resembles fine breadcrumbs. Add sufficient chilled water to make a soft, but not sticky, dough. Form into 8 dumplings and add them to the beef mixture.

18

4 Cover the pan and simmer for about 20 minutes until the dumplings are cooked – they should be light and fluffy.

Serve at once, accompanied by fresh vegetables and mashed potatoes.

STEAK AND KIDNEY PUDDING

Allow plenty of time when you begin to make this traditional savory dish, as it needs several hours to steam to perfection.

SERVES ❹

3 cups self-rising flour

1¼ cups shredded beef suet

¼ cup all-purpose flour

1 lb braising steak, trimmed and cut into 1 inch chunks

½ cup trimmed and chopped ox kidney

1 small onion, chopped

1 cup open-cap mushrooms, wiped and sliced

few drops of mushroom catsup or Worcestershire sauce

salt and pepper

1 Thoroughly grease a 5 cup pudding bowl with a little margarine.

2 Sift the self-rising flour and a pinch of salt into a large mixing bowl. Stir in the shredded beef suet and add sufficient chilled water to make a soft, but not sticky, dough.

3 On a lightly floured counter roll out about three quarters of the dough and use it to line the prepared greased pudding bowl.

4 Sprinkle the all-purpose flour onto a large plate and season. Roll the steak and kidney pieces, onion, and mushrooms in the flour, then put into the dough-lined bowl. Sprinkle with a few drops of mushroom catsup or Worcestershire sauce, then add just enough cold water to reach the top of the meat.

5 Roll out the remaining dough to form a lid for the pudding bowl. Moisten the edges and position over the meat

mixture, pressing the edges of the dough together well to seal them. Cover with a large piece of wax paper or foil and secure with string.

6 Put the pudding bowl in a steamer over a pan of gently boiling water and steam for about 4¹/₂ hours, adding more boiling water when necessary to prevent the steamer from boiling dry. Serve with carrots, cabbage or Brussels sprouts, and boiled or mashed potatoes.

BRAISED BRISKET OF BEEF

Brisket of beef is a delicious cut of meat, especially when slow-cooked in the oven. The red wine and juniper berries add a distinctive but subtle flavor.

SERVES 6

2 tbsp vegetable oil

2½ lb piece of brisket of beef, rolled and tied

8 oz small onions, halved

1¼ cups beef stock

1¼ cups red wine

2 bay leaves

6 juniper berries

1 tbsp chopped fresh parsley

2 tbsp cornstarch, blended with a little cold water

salt and pepper

1 Heat the vegetable oil in a large flameproof casserole. Add the piece of brisket and cook over a high heat, turning it to seal and brown on all sides.

2 Add the onions, beef stock, red wine, bay leaves, juniper berries, and parsley. Season to taste. Bring to the boil, then cover the casserole.

3 Place the casserole in a preheated oven at 325°F, and cook for about 2 hours until the meat is tender, basting it occasionally. Remove the brisket from the casserole and leave to rest for about 5 minutes.

4 Add the blended cornstarch to the gravy in the casserole and stir well. Bring to the boil over a low heat, stirring constantly until it is thickened and blended. Cook gently for 2 minutes.

Carve the meat and serve with the gravy, accompanied by potatoes and a selection of various fresh green vegetables.

ROAST LAMB WITH ONION SAUCE

Garlic and rosemary give a subtle flavor to roast lamb, which in this recipe is served with an onion sauce as a pleasant change to mint sauce or gravy.

SERVES ❻

3–3½ lb filet end leg of lamb

2 large garlic cloves, cut into slivers

sprigs of fresh rosemary

2 tbsp butter

sprigs of fresh rosemary to garnish

SAUCE

2 tbsp butter

1 large onion, chopped finely

¼ cup all-purpose flour

generous ¾ cup milk

⅔ cup lamb or vegetable stock

pinch of ground allspice

salt and pepper

1 Using a sharp knife, make small incisions over the surface of the lamb. Insert the slivers of garlic and some tiny sprigs of rosemary. Spread the butter over the lamb.

2 Transfer to a roasting pan and place in a preheated oven at 425°F. Roast for 30 minutes, then reduce the temperature to 350°F and cook for a further 1½–1¾ hours.

3 About 20 minutes before the end of the cooking time, make the onion sauce. Melt the butter in a pan and add the onion. Cook very gently over a low heat for about 10 minutes, until softened but not brown, stirring occasionally. Stir in the flour and cook gently for 1 minute, then add the milk and stock gradually, stirring well between each addition. Bring to the boil, stirring constantly until smooth and thickened. Add a pinch of allspice, and season.

Carve the lamb and serve with potatoes, vegetables, and the onion sauce. Garnish with sprigs of fresh rosemary.

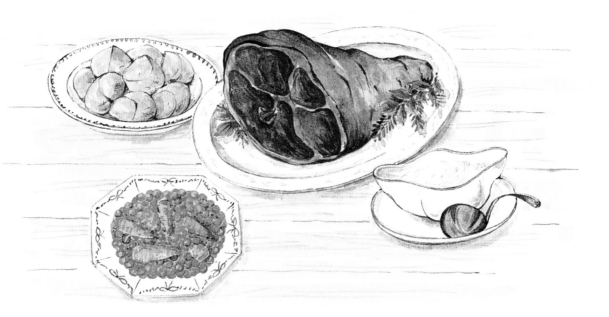

RABBIT CASSEROLE WITH MUSTARD AND BACON

SERVES 6

2 lb rabbit pieces

¼ cup all-purpose flour

2 tbsp butter

1 tbsp vegetable oil

½ cup chopped thick-cut bacon

6 oz shallots

2 celery stalks, sliced

1¼ cups dry white wine

⅔ cup chicken or vegetable stock

1 tbsp wholegrain mustard

1 bay leaf

salt and pepper

Rabbit makes a welcome change from other meats or poultry and tastes particularly good with this combination of white wine and bacon.

1 Rinse the rabbit pieces and pat dry with paper towels. Dust on all sides with the flour.

2 Heat the butter and oil in a large skillet and add the rabbit pieces. Cook over a fairly high heat to brown and seal them, then transfer to a large casserole.

3 Add the bacon to the skillet and cook until the fat begins to run, then transfer to the casserole. Fry the shallots gently in the bacon fat, then add to the casserole with the celery.

4 Pour the white wine into the skillet and bring to the boil, stirring well to combine with the pan juices. Pour into the casserole with the stock. Stir in the wholegrain mustard and season to taste. Add the bay leaf.

5 Cover the casserole and cook in a preheated oven at 375°F for 1½–2 hours until very tender. Remove the bay leaf and serve immediately.

POT-ROASTED CHICKEN

SERVES 4

2 tbsp butter

1 tbsp vegetable oil

½ cup chopped smoked bacon

3–3½ lb chicken

1 large onion, sliced

1 large carrot, sliced

1 small lemon, halved

1¼ cups dry white wine

1¼ cups chicken stock

small bunch of fresh herbs, tied in a bundle

2 tbsp cornstarch, blended with a little cold water

Pot-roasted chicken is exceptionally succulent, and a lemon placed in the cavity of the bird gives it a lovely flavor. For a slightly different flavor, use red wine instead of white and add 1 cup button mushrooms to the casserole.

1 Heat the butter and oil in a large flameproof casserole and fry the bacon until the fat runs. Remove the bacon and set it aside.

2 Put the chicken in the casserole and fry it over a fairly high heat, turning it over to brown on all sides. Remove the chicken and set it aside.

3 Fry the sliced onion and carrot in the casserole for 3–4 minutes, until lightly browned.

4 Push the lemon halves into the cavity of the chicken and return to the casserole with the bacon. Pour in the wine and stock and bring to the boil. Then turn off the heat, add the bundle of herbs, and cover the casserole with a piece of foil.

5 Place the casserole in a preheated oven at 375°F, and cook for 1½–2 hours until tender, basting occasionally with the stock.

28

6 When the chicken is cooked, remove it from the casserole, draining it well. Discard the herbs and lemon halves.

7 Add the blended cornstarch to the cooking liquid, stirring to mix. Cook over a gentle heat, stirring constantly until thickened and blended. Cook for 1 minute, then serve with the chicken.

PIGGIES IN THE HOLE

Serve this straight from the oven, all puffed up and golden brown. The mushroom and onion gravy complements it perfectly.

SERVES ④

1 cup all-purpose flour

½ tsp dried thyme

1 large egg

1¼ cups milk

2 tbsp vegetable oil

1 lb pork sausages

GRAVY

1 tbsp butter or margarine

1 small onion, chopped finely

½ cup thinly sliced button mushrooms

scant 2 cups vegetable or chicken stock

2 tbsp cornstarch blended with a little cold water

salt and pepper

1 Sift the flour and a pinch of salt into a large mixing bowl. Add the herbs, egg, and milk and, using a balloon whisk or electric hand mixer, beat together to make a smooth batter. Set aside for 10–15 minutes before using.

2 Meanwhile, pour the oil into a roasting pan and arrange the sausages side by side in the base. Place in a preheated oven at 425°F, for 10 minutes so that the oil gets very hot.

3 Remove from the oven, pour in the batter quickly, and return to the oven. (It is important to pour the batter into very hot oil and return it to the oven immediately.) Cook for 25–30 minutes until the batter is well risen and golden brown.

4 While this is cooking, make the gravy. Melt the margarine or butter in a pan and fry the onion gently for about 8–10 minutes until well browned.

30

Add the mushrooms and cook for a further 2 minutes. Pour in the stock and bring to the boil, then reduce the heat and simmer gently for 10 minutes. Add the blended cornstarch and cook, stirring, for about 2 minutes, until thickened and smooth. Season to taste. Divide the cooked dish into 4 portions and serve with the gravy and some fresh vegetables.

PORK, SAUSAGES, AND BEANS

SERVES ❹

3 oz navy beans, soaked
overnight

3 oz black-eye peas, soaked
overnight

12 oz belly pork, de-rinded

12 oz pork sausages

1 tbsp vegetable oil

1 large onion, chopped

1 large carrot, chopped

2 cups ham, chicken, or
vegetable stock

2 tbsp dark muscovado or
molasses sugar

2 tbsp tomato paste

1 tbsp chopped fresh herbs

2 tsp chopped fresh ginger root

14 oz can tomatoes

2 tbsp cornstarch mixed with a
little cold water

This warming casserole of belly pork, pork sausages, and beans is farmhouse cookery at its best – a simple and inexpensive dish full of flavor and goodness.

1 Drain the beans and rinse well with fresh water. Place the beans in a large pan of water, bring to the boil and boil rapidly for 10 minutes. Drain.

2 Cut the meat into 1 inch cubes. Twist the sausages in the middle and snip them in half.

3 Heat the oil in a large flameproof casserole and add the belly pork, cooking over a high heat until beginning to brown on all sides. Add the sausages and fry gently for a few more minutes until browned. Add the onion and carrot and cook for 2–3 minutes to soften. Add the stock, sugar, tomato paste, herbs, and ginger, and chop up and stir in the tomatoes. Season to taste.

4 Cover the casserole, place in a preheated oven at 325°F and cook for

2–2¹/2 hours until the pork is tender and the beans are soft. Stir in the blended cornstarch.

Return to the oven for a further 5 minutes to cook and thicken before serving.

CRISPY-TOPPED FISH PIE

A crisp and golden topping of cheesy potatoes conceals a layer of cod in a creamy parsley sauce in this easy and tasty fish recipe.

SERVES 4

- 3 tbsp butter or margarine
- 1½ lb potatoes
- 1 bunch scallions, trimmed and chopped finely
- ⅓ cup all-purpose flour
- 1¼ cups milk
- 1 tbsp chopped fresh parsley
- 1½ lb cod or haddock, skinned, boned, and cut into chunks
- 1 egg
- ⅔ cup plain yogurt
- 1 cup shredded sharp cheese
- salt and black pepper

1 Grease a 1½ quart ovenproof dish with a little of the butter or margarine.

2 Cook the potatoes in plenty of boiling, lightly salted water until just tender. Drain and slice.

3 Melt the remaining butter or margarine in a pan and fry the scallions gently until softened. Remove the pan from the heat and stir in the flour. Then cook over a low heat for 1 minute and add the milk gradually. Bring to the boil, stirring constantly. Cook until smooth and thick. Add the parsley and season to taste. Stir in the fish.

4 Transfer the mixture to the greased ovenproof dish and arrange the sliced potatoes over the top in an overlapping layer.

5 Beat together the egg and yogurt. Add half the cheese and season to taste. Pour over the potatoes and sprinkle with

the remaining cheese. Bake in a preheated oven at 375°F for 25–30 minutes until set and golden brown.

Serve at once, with lightly cooked fresh vegetables or a salad.

TROUT WITH LEMON AND HERB MARINADE

SERVES 4

4 trout, cleaned and gutted

finely grated rind of 1 large lemon

4 tbsp lemon juice

4 tbsp olive oil

1 large garlic clove, crushed

1 tbsp chopped fresh marjoram

1 tbsp chopped fresh parsley (flat leaf or curly)

salt and pepper

Fish lends itself well to simple methods of cooking, as this recipe for trout marinated in a lemon, garlic, and herb mixture proves.

1 Rinse the trout well, then use a sharp knife to make 2 or 3 slashes on each side of the fish, in the thickest part of the flesh. Place in a shallow, non-metallic container.

2 Mix together the lemon rind and juice, olive oil, garlic, marjoram, and parsley. Season to taste, then pour the mixture over the fish. Cover and leave to marinate for 2–3 hours.

3 Place the fish on a preheated hot broiler rack and cook for about 5 minutes each side, basting frequently with the lemon and herb mixture. The fish is cooked when the flesh is opaque and flakes easily.

Serve at once, accompanied by baby potatoes and a selection of fresh vegetables, or a green salad.

Trout with Lemon and Herbs

SALMON FISH CAKES WITH DILL SAUCE

Fish cakes take on a new meaning with this special recipe, which uses fresh salmon and dill. Smoked haddock or cod can be used for a more economical version.

SERVES ❹

1 lb potatoes, cut into large chunks

12 oz salmon fillets or steaks

sprigs of fresh dill or parsley

2 tsp white wine vinegar

¼ cup butter

⅔ cup light cream

2 tsp lemon juice

2 tsp chopped fresh dill or parsley

¼ cup plus 2 tbsp all-purpose flour

1 egg, separated

1½ cups fresh white breadcrumbs

butter and vegetable oil

salt and pepper

1 Cook the potatoes in plenty of boiling, lightly salted water until tender. Drain well and mash them.

2 While the potatoes are cooking, place the salmon in a shallow pan with the sprigs of dill or parsley and the vinegar. Pour in just enough water to cover. Place the pan over a low heat and simmer gently to poach the fish. When cooked, the fish should be opaque and will flake easily. Drain well, reserving the poaching liquid. Flake the fish with a fork, removing any skin and bones.

3 Mix together the potatoes and fish with 2 tbsp of the butter, 3 tbsp of the light cream, the lemon juice, and 1 tsp of the chopped dill or parsley. Season to taste.

4 Form the mixture into 8 cakes and dust with ¼ cup of the flour. Beat the egg white in a shallow bowl with 1 tbsp cold water. Put the breadcrumbs on a separate plate. Dip the fish cakes in the egg white, then coat with the

breadcrumbs. Fry in butter and vegetable oil until cooked and golden brown, about 4–5 minutes on each side.

5 To make the sauce, put the remaining butter, cream, dill or parsley, egg yolk, flour, and 4 tbsp of the poaching liquid into a small pan. Heat, stirring constantly with a balloon whisk, until thickened and smooth.

Serve with the fish cakes.

GOLDEN POTATO CAKES

Served with sizzling bacon and fresh eggs for breakfast, these potato cakes are delicious.

1 Mash the potatoes with 3 tbsp of the butter, then beat well until smooth, using an electric hand mixer for the best results. Add the egg and ½ cup of the flour, beating well until thoroughly blended. Season well to taste.

2 On a lightly floured counter, use a rolling pin to press and roll the mixture out gently until it forms a circle about 10 inches in diameter. Cut into large wedges and dust with the remaining flour.

3 Heat the oil with the remaining butter in a large heavy-based skillet.
Add the potato cakes and cook over a gentle heat for about 4–5 minutes. Turn over carefully and cook the other side until golden brown. Drain on paper towels before serving.

BAKED STUFFED ONIONS

Use mildly flavored onions to make this economical recipe. Be sure to make full use of the oven by cooking another dish at the same time – why not bake some potatoes to serve with the onions?

1 Grease an ovenproof dish with butter.

2 Put the onions into a large pan of lightly salted water. Bring to the boil, reduce the heat, and cook for 15 minutes. Drain and cool slightly, then hollow out the centers and chop them finely.

3 Fry the bacon in a medium skillet until the fat runs. Add the ground beef, chopped onion, and mushrooms and cook for 8–10 minutes over a medium heat, stirring frequently. Remove from the heat and stir in the breadcrumbs and herbs. Season to taste.

4 Stand the whole onions in the greased ovenproof dish. Pack the ground beef mixture into the centers and pour the stock around them. Place in a preheated oven at 350°F, and bake for 1½–2 hours until tender.

42

VEGETABLE PATTIES

Excellent served with chops, bacon, ham, or sausages, this delicious recipe is an ideal way of using up leftover potatoes. A couple of teaspoons of wholegrain mustard can be added to the mixture.

1 Put the onion and cabbage into a large pan with a little boiling, lightly salted water. Cover and cook for about 5–6 minutes, until tender. Drain the vegetables well.

2 While the vegetables are cooking, beat the cooked potatoes and butter together until smooth, using either a wooden spoon or, preferably, an electric hand mixer for best results. Add the chives or parsley, then mix in the cooked onion and cabbage.

3 Season well, then divide the mixture into 8 and form each piece into a rectangular patty. Sift the flour onto a plate and use to coat the patties lightly.

4 Heat the vegetable oil in a large skillet and fry the patties gently for about 4 minutes on each side, until cooked and golden brown. Drain on paper towels and serve at once.

GREEN TOMATO CHUTNEY

MAKES 3lb

2 lb green tomatoes, chopped

2 cups chopped onions

8 oz apples, peeled, cored, and chopped

⅔ cup golden raisins

1¼ cups light malt vinegar

1 cup light muscovado sugar

2 tsp grated fresh ginger root

1 tsp mustard seeds

2 tsp salt

½ tsp pepper

Make the most of the last of the summer tomatoes in this robust chutney. It's the ideal accompaniment to fine Cheddar cheese or homecooked ham.

1 Sterilize 3 x 1 lb glass jars by one of the following methods: wash the jars in hot soapy water and rinse in boiling water, turn upside down on a clean dish towel to dry, and then place in a cool oven for about 15 minutes; or wash in the dishwasher and remove just before filling; or quarter fill the jars with water, microwave on full power, then pour out the water and leave the jars to dry upside down on a dish towel.

2 Put the tomatoes, onions, apples, golden raisins, and vinegar into a pan. Bring to the boil, reduce the heat and simmer for about 5 minutes. Stir in the sugar and allow to dissolve over a low heat. Add the ginger, mustard seeds, salt, and pepper.

3 Simmer, uncovered, stirring occasionally until the mixture becomes thick and

46

pulpy. The chutney must have quite a thick consistency, as it thickens only slightly as it cools.

4 Pot the chutney in warmed, sterilized jars. Seal and label.

SUMMER PUDDING

This beautiful dessert is a treat served in the summer months when the soft fruit you need is available. Serve it with a bowl of fresh whipped cream or natural fromage frais.

SERVES 6

1⅓ cups strawberries, hulled

1⅓ cups raspberries

1 cup redcurrants

1 cup blackcurrants

½ cup superfine sugar

6–7 medium-thick slices white bread, crusts removed

whipped cream or fromage frais to serve

1 Grease a 3½ cup pudding bowl with a little butter.

2 Rinse the fruit, then slice the strawberries and put them into a pan. Add the raspberries to the pan. Using a fork carefully strip the redcurrants and blackcurrants from their stalks, then add to the pan containing the other fruit with the sugar.

3 Heat gently so that the sugar dissolves and the juice begins to run from the fruit, about 3–4 minutes. Remove the pan from the heat.

4 Line the bowl with the bread, reserving some for the top. Press the edges together and use small pieces of bread to fill up any gaps.

5 Reserve 4 tbsp of the juice from the fruit. Pour the fruit and remaining juice into the prepared bowl, and cover with the reserved bread. Place a saucer or small plate on top of the bowl to fit as closely as possible, then place a heavy weight on top. Refrigerate for 6–8 hours, or overnight.

6 When ready to serve, turn the pudding out onto a large plate. Use the reserved fruit juice to spoon over any patches of bread that remain white.

Cut into wedges and serve with whipped cream or natural fromage frais.

APPLE AND BLACKBERRY PIE

Apples and blackberries are a winning combination. Try them in this single-crust pie, excellent served with cream, custard, ice cream, or yogurt.

SERVES 6

1 lb apples, peeled, cored and chopped

2 tsp lemon juice

2 cups blackberries

½ cup soft brown sugar

1½ cups self-rising flour

pinch of salt

½ tsp ground cinnamon

¼ cup butter or margarine

1 egg, beaten

3 tbsp milk

brown sugar crystals, for sprinkling

1 Grease a 1½ quart deep ovenproof dish with a little butter.

2 Put the apples into a pan with a little water and the lemon juice. Remove any stalks or leaves from the blackberries and add to the pan with ⅓ cup of the soft brown sugar. Simmer gently over a low heat for 10 minutes. Allow the mixture to cool slightly before spooning it into the prepared greased ovenproof dish.

3 Sift the flour, salt, and cinnamon into a mixing bowl and stir in the remaining soft brown sugar. Rub in the butter or margarine with your fingertips until the mixture resembles fine breadcrumbs. Beat the egg and milk together, then add enough to the flour mixture to make a soft, but not sticky, dough. Knead lightly for a few moments, then chill for 5–10 minutes.

4 Roll out the dough to fit the top of the dish. Lift onto the dish, trim the edges and use any

trimmings to make leaves for decorating the top. Brush the dough with any remaining egg and milk mixture to glaze. Sprinkle with sugar crystals.

5 Place in a preheated oven at 400°F and bake for 20–25 minutes until cooked and light golden brown.

FARMHOUSE CURD TART

Fresh dairy ingredients are the making of this lovely lemon-flavored cheesecake tart – a favorite dessert for those who prefer their puddings not too sweet.

1 Sift the flour and salt into a large mixing bowl. Cut the butter or margarine into pieces, add to the flour, and rub in with your fingertips until the mixture resembles fine breadcrumbs. Stir in enough chilled water to make a firm dough. Knead lightly for a few moments, then cover in plastic wrap and refrigerate for about 10 minutes.

2 Roll out the chilled dough on a lightly floured counter, and use to line a 9 inch pie plate or flan dish. Prick the base with a fork and line with foil. Place in a preheated oven at 425°F, and bake for 10 minutes. Remove from the oven, take off the foil and allow the pastry to cool a little. Reduce the heat to 350°F.

3 To make the filling, beat together the eggs and cream. Add the cottage cheese, superfine sugar, vanilla extract, white raisins, and

lemon rind. Pour into the pastry case and sprinkle with nutmeg.

4 Bake the tart for about 35 minutes, until the filling has set and turned a light golden brown. Allow to cool slightly before serving with a pitcher of light cream.

CHEESE AND FRESH HERB SCONES

Hot from the oven, these delicious scones are fragrant with the aroma of fresh herbs and cheese. Serve them while still warm, split and spread with butter.

MAKES 16

4 cups self-rising flour

pinch of salt

½ cup butter or margarine

1½ cups shredded sharp Cheddar cheese

2 tbsp chopped fresh mixed herbs, such as chervil, chives, marjoram, mint, parsley, sage, and thyme.

2 eggs

1¼ cups milk

1 Brush 2 baking trays with a little oil.

2 Sift the flour and salt together into a large mixing bowl, then rub in the butter or margarine with your fingertips until the mixture resembles fine breadcrumbs. Stir in 1 cup of the shredded cheese and the herbs.

3 Beat together the eggs and milk, then add most of the liquid to the cheese mixture. Draw together to make a soft, but not sticky, dough and knead lightly for a few moments until smooth.

4 Roll the dough out on a lightly floured counter to a thickness of about 1 inch. Using a 2 inch pastry cutter stamp out 16 rounds. Place on the baking trays, brush with the remaining egg and milk mixture to glaze , and sprinkle the remaining cheese on top.

54

5 Place in a preheated oven at 425°F, and bake until risen and golden brown, about 10–12 minutes. Transfer to a wire rack to cool slightly. Serve warm, spread with butter.

RAISIN DROP SCONES

MAKES 18

1 cup self-rising flour

pinch of salt

1 heaped tbsp soft brown sugar

1 egg

1 tsp vanilla extract

½ tsp finely grated orange rind

⅔ cup plain yogurt

2 tbsp milk

3 tbsp golden raisins or raisins

few drops of vegetable oil

Drop scones, or Scotch pancakes as they are sometimes known, get their name from the way that the batter is dropped onto a hot griddle – although a heavy-based skillet can easily be used instead.

1 Sift the flour and salt into a mixing bowl. Stir in the sugar. Add the egg, vanilla extract, orange rind, yogurt, and milk and beat together using a wire whisk until the batter is smooth. Stir in the golden raisins or raisins.

2 Heat a griddle or heavy-based skillet, adding just a few drops of oil to grease the surface. Turn the heat to low. Drop tablespoonfuls of the batter onto the hot surface, allowing space for each spoonful to spread out a little. When air-bubbles appear on the surface of the scones after about 2 minutes, flip each scone over and cook for a further 2 minutes. Using a pancake turner, lift them out onto paper towels or a clean dish towel, then cook the remaining batter, adding a few more drops of oil to the pan if necessary.

These are best served warm, spread with butter.

SERVES **8**

2 cups wholewheat self-rising
flour

pinch of salt

½ tsp ground apple pie spice

⅔ cup light muscovado or
molasses sugar

⅓ cup butter or margarine

2 eggs

½ cup milk

3 tbsp dates, chopped

3 tbsp ready-to-eat dried
apricots, chopped

3 tbsp golden raisins

WHOLEWHEAT FRUIT BREAD

*This easy-to-make fruit bread is best served
in slices spread with butter, and is ideal for taking
on picnics.*

1 Grease a 2 lb loaf pan with a little vegetable oil. Line with baking parchment.

2 Sift the flour, salt, and apple pie spice into a mixing bowl, adding any bits of bran that remain in the strainer. Stir in the sugar, then rub in the butter or margarine with your fingertips until the mixture resembles fine breadcrumbs.

3 Beat together the eggs and milk, and add to the mixture with the dates, apricots, and golden raisins, stirring well to mix thoroughly.

4 Turn the mixture into the prepared pan and level the surface. Place in a preheated oven at 325°F, and bake for about 1 hour 10 minutes until risen and golden brown.

To test if the bread is cooked, insert a skewer into the center – it should come out clean.

5 Cool the bread in the pan for 10 minutes, then transfer to a wire rack to cool completely.

BLACKCURRANT PRESERVE

MAKES 6lb

8 cups blackcurrants

3½ cups water

6 firmly packed cups granulated sugar

Make the most of soft summer fruit with this wonderful preserve. Blackcurrants are ideal because they have a high pectin content, which helps the preserve to set.

1 Sterilize 6 x 1 lb glass jars (see page 46).

2 Check over the fruit to remove any stalks and leaves, but avoid washing the fruit unless really necessary.

3 Put the fruit into a preserving pan or other very large pan with the water. Simmer gently over a low heat for 30–40 minutes to soften the fruit and release the pectin.

4 Add the sugar to the black-white raisins and allow it to dissolve, stirring occasionally. Bring to the boil and boil rapidly until setting point is reached (see below) – about 15–20 minutes. Skim off any scum, but not foam, near the end of the cooking time.

5 To test for setting-point, spoon a little of the mixture onto a cold saucer and cool it quickly. Push it with your finger – it should crinkle on the surface, but should not be stiff. Double-check by putting a drop of the

60

cooled preserve on the end of your finger. If it does not fall off, it is ready.

6 Pot the preserve in the warmed, sterilized jars, seal, and label. It will set as it cools.

LEMON SPREAD

MAKES 1 ½ lb
4 eggs
1 firmly packed cup superfine sugar
finely grated rind of 2 large lemons
½ cup lemon juice
1 cup unsalted butter, melted

Fresh homemade lemon spread is a real treat, especially when spread generously on crusty new bread. Remember to refrigerate and eat within 3 weeks – although there should be no problem in doing that!

1 Sterilize 2 x 12 oz glass jars (see page 46).

2 Whisk together the eggs, sugar, lemon rind, and juice in a heatproof mixing bowl. Add the warm melted butter and stir together.

3 Set the bowl over a pan of gently simmering water and stir with a wooden spoon until the mixture thickens, about 10–15 minutes. Check that it is thick enough by lifting the wooden spoon a little and drizzling the lemon spread over the surface of the mixture – it should be thick enough to leave a trail. The lemon spread will thicken more as it cools.

4 Pot the lemon spread in warmed sterilized jars. Seal and label. When completely cool, store in the refrigerator.

INDEX